Preface

Samanta's Journey of Hope is the account of one child's experience as an orphan on her path to finding a home and prosperous future. This is a story of hope – for the child, for her adoptive parents, and for all those wondering how they can help children who have not yet found a loving home. In this account, we hear from Samanta through the voice of her parents, who traveled to Ecuador to find their daughter. This story is an inspiration to anyone who cares about children, not only to those involved in the adoption process. Samanta's parents desire that the positive energy drawn from their wonderful experience can bring hope and help to other orphaned children around the world.

authorHOUSE®

AuthorHouse™
1663 Liberty Drive
Bloomington, IN 47403
www.authorhouse.com
Phone: 1-800-839-8640

First published by AuthorHouse 5/22/2009

ISBN: 978-1-4389-6550-5 (sc)

Library of Congress Control Number: 2009904949

Idea and Realization: Urs and Evelyne Ribary
Illustrations: Ursula Abplanalp
Text and Drawings: Magda Blau
Translated from German by Michaela Egger

Printed in the United States of America
Bloomington, Indiana

This book is printed on acid-free paper.

All proceeds from this book will be donated to the
Samanta S. Ribary Foundation at
<www.samanta-ribary-foundation.org>

Samanta's
Journey of Hope

To Samanta
and all those who open their hearts to children in need.

My name is Samanta. I was born high up in the mountains of Ecuador.
I like to gaze at the blue sky. I watch puffy white clouds drifting above the
mountaintops. "Where are they traveling to?" I wonder. The clouds just keep
floating past me all day long...

But wait, what is this I see? A smudge of blue amidst the white clouds? It looks like a flower! A blue flower, peeking out at me. I see it again and again. Sometimes I can make out only its petals, but often the whole beautiful flower. I want to ask her: "Dear Flower, why are the clouds drifting by so fast? Where are they drifting to? Dear Flower, you are so wonderful. Please stay beside me; please don't ever forget to shine on me and protect me." I can feel its response in my heart: "Samanta, I will be with you wherever you go, because I live in the sky, and the blue sky is everywhere!"

As I am sitting in the grass gazing up at the sky, a Paradise Bird lands gently on the rocks right next to me to keep me company. He sings me a tale about flying up far into the sky to greet the Blue Flower. This Paradise Bird is a wondrous bird and all knowing. He glides over mountains and valleys and can see everything that happens in the world. So I ask of him: "Dear Paradise Bird, please, could you bring me the Blue Flower? Here in the mountains I am one of so many children. But if I have it by me, I'll never feel alone again."

"We shall change this!" Paradise Bird promises me. "I will bring you the Blue Flower you desire and it will bring you luck as you are about to embark on a big journey. It will become so small that you can carry it with you in a locket you will be wearing around your neck." He flaps his wings and disappears into the sky. When he returns, he explains further: "Samanta, the flower will guide you on your upcoming journey; you must promise, however, that once you have found your happiness on earth, you will return it so that it can bring luck to many more children."

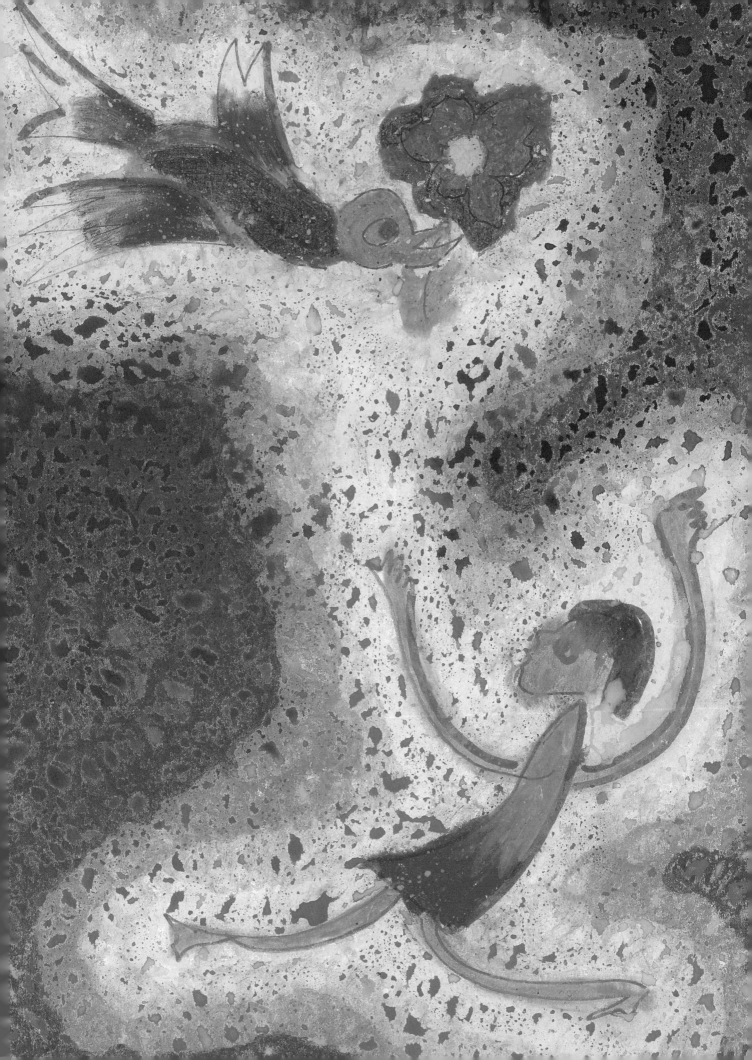

I am so excited: "Of course, Paradise Bird. I will return the Blue Flower to you. But please bring it to me quickly, because my tribe will be traveling to the market very soon. I don't know what will happen there, but with Blue Flower by my side to protect me I am no longer worried."

Paradise Bird returns, as promised, carrying the Blue Flower in his beak. Like a magician he folds it so that it fits into Samanta's locket. Around them, looking on in amazement, are alpacas, sheep and cows. They are Samanta's friends, and they help her community to survive by providing them with milk, meat, and wool to make warm clothes for the cold in the mountains.

As Samanta is carried off, on a woman's back, she asks Blue Flower: "Where am I going? Why is this woman carrying me on her back? Where do I belong? Where is my home?" And the Blue Flower reassures her: "Don't worry, Samanta, my child. You are safe. You are embarking on your journey of hope."

There are loud voices everywhere. People are shouting back and forth to one another. The market is a busy place. From all directions, people are rushing to the center. Children, food and clothing items are bundled together with cloths and bound to people's backs. Big and small, young and old – they are all headed down to the market, a hike of several hours through the mountains. All the Indios have are the goods they create with their own hands. Samanta's kinfolk have been working very hard and hope to sell their goods at the market, so they can buy food to eat.

Paradise Bird circles above the crowds and observes. He follows them through the mountains and into the valley. Samanta does not want to take her eyes off Paradise Bird, though she can recognize him even when he is flying way ahead with the other birds. She knows he is there with her, watching over her and anxiously waiting to tell her more about her future. Samanta checks to see whether her locket has come loose – but the Blue Flower is still there.

The market is bustling and people are pushing past one another. They are talking loudly, laughing and joking, as they try to sell their wares and goods.

Samanta feels very tired. But she knows Paradise Bird and Blue Flower are watching her, so she closes her eyes.

Suddenly Samanta opens her eyes, but she does not know where she is. She is lying in a crib in a small room with many other children. She asks the two other little girls in her crib: "Where am I? This is not where I fell asleep at the market among my kinfolk. Who brought me here? Do I have to stay here without the mountains, without the blue sky, without my friends the alpacas? There are no colorful rocks here to play with. Is this supposed to be my new home?"

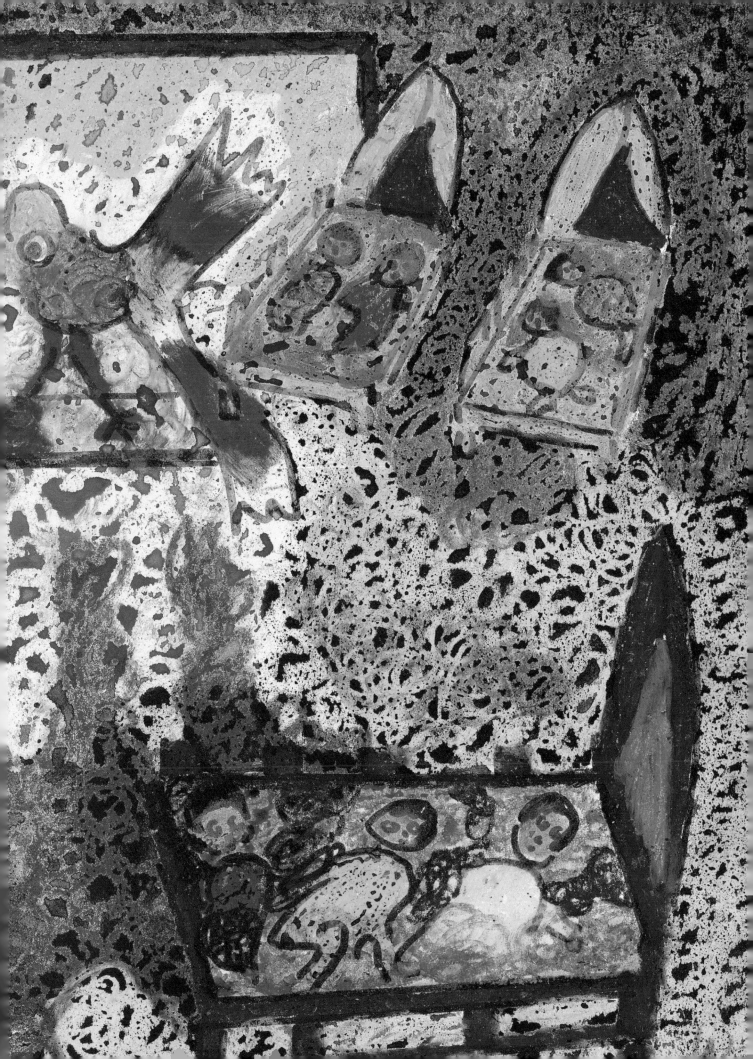

"Paradise Bird – where am I? Blue Flower, are you still there in my locket? Oh, I'm so glad you are here with me, Paradise Bird."

Paradise Bird tells her: "Don't you worry, dear Samanta, you will not be here long. Your journey will continue!"

Paradise Bird sings her his most beautiful song and Samanta understands that very soon, two people will come who will love her very much.

Samanta has been in a caring orphanage for several weeks. She shares her room with many other children. Each one of them longs for his or her own home. Samanta feels so very sad.

But Paradise Bird whispers to her: "Be patient Samanta! They will be here very soon!"

Samanta's big round eyes get even bigger and begin to glow. A man and a woman are standing at the door, crying because they are so happy to see little Samanta. The woman's dress is covered with blue flowers and the man has a blue flower peeking out of his shirt pocket.

Samanta looks all around her; she is so astonished. She feels deep in her heart that these are two people who have come to her to love her very much. Two people who love her and whom she can love!

"The woman leans over my bed and reaches for me to gently pick me up and hold me close to her warm body. For three weeks, these two wonderful people play with me – they take me into the garden where Paradise Bird sits on a tree branch and sings his joyful songs for us. Today he's singing a beautiful song with a secretive melody."

Samanta can make out a story about a long journey to a far off place.

All her wishes that she has shared with Blue Flower will come true. Now Samanta has parents who love her and who will take her to their home – the place that will soon become Samanta's home as well. Her parents are also very grateful, namely to all those, who showed them the way to find Samanta. They too, will have their wishes fulfilled.

All bags are packed and a long journey is upon them. Paradise Bird does not cease his joyous singing. He wants to sing as loudly as possible so that he can help many other children who are waiting for parents who will love them and give them a new home. Samanta returns Blue Flower to Paradise Bird, so that he can show it to all the other children to give them hope. Paradise Bird will call upon others to take the children out of the orphanage and bring them into their new homes where they can feel loved and secure.

Samanta climbs into an airplane with her parents and they fly for many hours. Paradise Bird flaps his wings alongside the airplane, accompanying them. Anywhere one could hear Paradise Bird sing his song of hope, which tells the story of two loving people who have opened their hearts, to spread joy and good fortune. He will show many other parents, who generously carry love in their hearts, the path to their own happiness.

Samanta lives with her parents in North America. She knows her parents will always be there to give her love, warmth and security. They are all very happy together.

All over the world, children can find a home where they feel loved and secure.

To this day, Samanta still looks up at the sky for Blue Flower and she still hears Paradise Bird's song.

Samanta never has to feel alone again !

Epilogue

This book is based on a true story. Samanta was found at the age of two months and spent eight months in an orphanage in Ecuador. Samanta does not know her biological parents. At the age of ten months, Samanta was adopted by the Swiss-American couple Evelyne and Urs, with whom she lives in North America.

Samanta is a precious, content, and curious child, who loves to laugh. Samanta and her parents feel very happy that they have found one another.

Samanta's positive aura has inspired the birth of the philanthropic Samanta S. Ribary Foundation, which provides assistance and support to orphans and children in need.

<www.samanta-ribary-foundation.org>

CPSIA information can be obtained at www.ICGtesting.com
Printed in the USA
LVIW01n0942130515
438263LV00005B/13